My First Book of Jokes

illustrated by Mark Guthrie

A Scholastic Australia Book

To Alex, Isabella and Jamie,
who make me laugh. No joke!—MG

Scholastic Australia
345 Pacific Highway Lindfield NSW 2070
An imprint of Scholastic Australia Pty Limited
PO Box 579 Gosford NSW 2250
ABN 11 000 614 577
www.scholastic.com.au

Part of the Scholastic Group
Sydney • Auckland • New York • Toronto • London • Mexico City
• New Delhi • Hong Kong • Buenos Aires • Puerto Rico

Published by Scholastic Australia in 2013.
Text copyright © Scholastic Australia, 2013.
Illustrations copyright © Mark Guthrie, 2013.

All rights reserved. No part of this publication may be reproduced or transmitted in any form or by any means, electronic or mechanical, including photocopying, recording, storage in an information retrieval system, or otherwise, without the prior written permission of the publisher, unless specifically permitted under the Australian Copyright Act 1968 as amended.

National Library of Australia Cataloguing-in-Publication entry:

Title:	My first book of jokes / illustrated by Mark Guthrie.
ISBN:	9781742837925 (pbk.)
Target Audience:	For primary school age.
Subjects:	Australian wit and humor.
	Wit and humor, Juvenile.
	Australia—Juvenile humor.
Dewey Number:	A828.402

Printed by Tien Wah Press, Malaysia.

Scholastic Australia's policy, in association with Tien Wah Press, is to use papers that are renewable and made efficiently from wood grown in sustainable forests, so as to minimise its environmental footprint.

10 9 8 7 6 5 4 3 2 1   13 14 15 16 17 / 1

What do you call a crocodile wearing a watch?

A tick-tockadile.

TICK TOCK

TICK TOCK

Why did the chicken cross the showground?

To get to the other ride!

What do you call a billabong during the winter?

A chillabong.

What do you call criminals robbing
a jewellery store?

Knickers!

What did the platypus say after she got some new lipstick?

Put it on my bill please.

Where do sick horses go?

To horsepital.

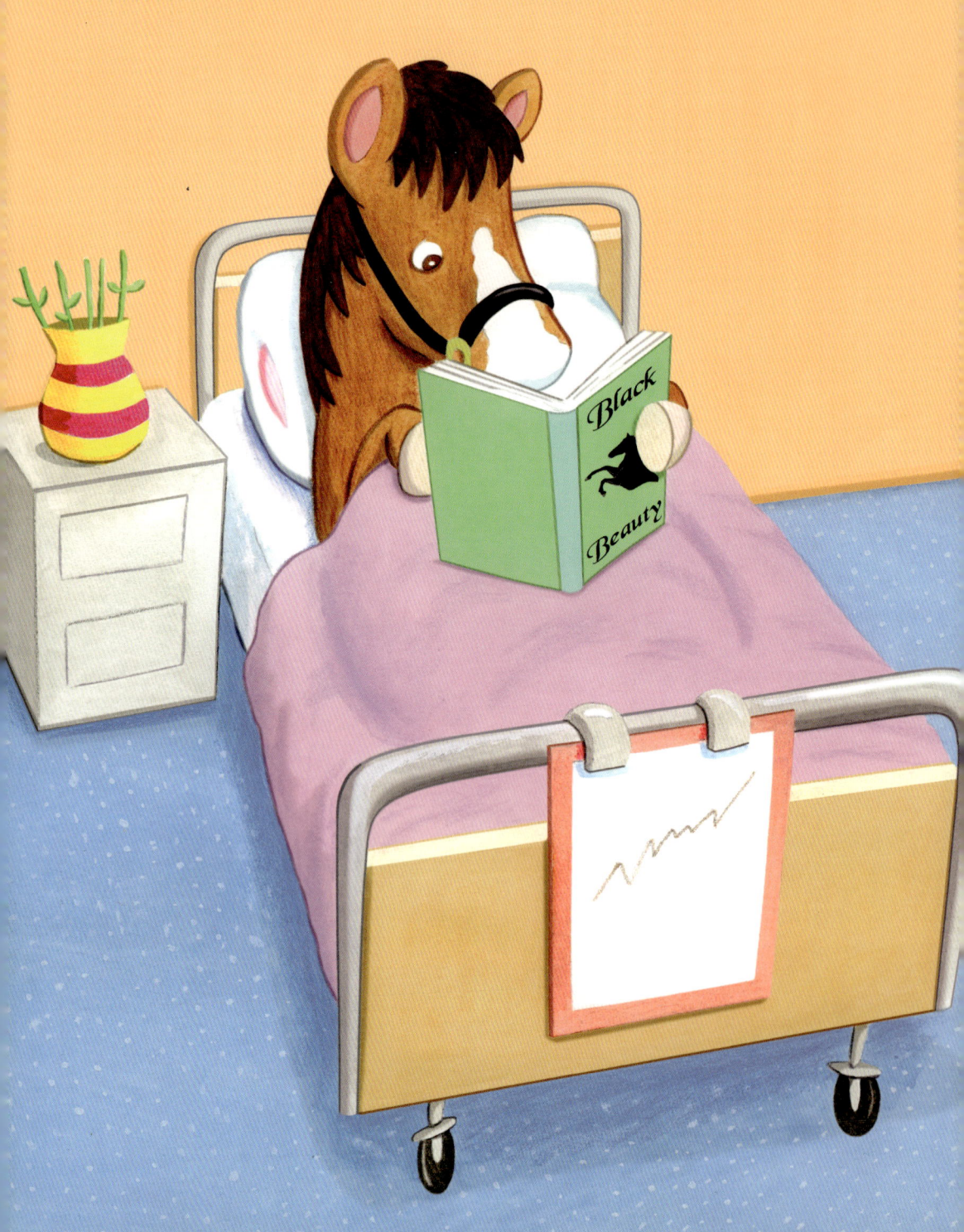

Did you hear about the naughty koala?

He decided to turn over a new leaf.

Why aren't bananas lonely?

Because they come in bunches!

What type of long-handled brush will always come back?

A broomerang.

Clean your room, it's a pig sty.
Mum xx

Why did the plumber get upset?

His job was going down the toilet.

What kind of monster sticks to the end of your finger?

A bogey monster!

What do cows like to eat for brekkie?

Moo-sli.

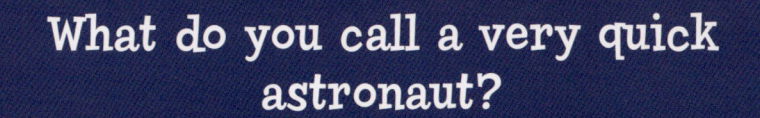

What do you call a very quick astronaut?

A fastronaut.

What do rainclouds wear under their clothes?

Thunderpants!

Why did the kookaburra sit on the clock?

So he would be on time!

school →